NO HUMAN IS LI
BY
LANGAT EMMANUEL

INTRODUCTION

It is kind of an interesting thought when we think about the world's heroes and heroines of all times together with the struggle they had to go through. From time to time, many books have been written trying to capture every moment of these individual's lives. That being said, it is a mere fact that we live in midst of heroes and heroines even in the present day. Talk of celebrities, to footballers, to musicians, to athletes, to world-class political leaders and successful entrepreneurs, there are individuals in the history whose memories will be permanently printed in the minds of generations to generations for many years.

What is encouraging though about these individuals, is that most of them started from very humble backgrounds. We are however just going to pick a few of them, from ages in the history. Right from the time of the famous Hellen Keller to even the latest of the most celebrated heroes like Bill Gates, Barrack Obama, Nancy Pelosi, Taylor Swift and Eliud Kipchoge, who has proofed to the entire human race that no human is limited.

DEDICATION
I dedicate this book to Eliud Kipchoge.
When you run, you inspire the world.

EARLY LIFE

As the saying goes, 'it is normal for one to be born a child, but it is not normal for one to remain a child'. I'd like to compare the life of a child to that of a tree. A seedling grows to a giant tree depending on the soil's nutrients and other environmental factors like rainfall and so is a life of a child. However, in most occasions, many of us have often found ourselves in different type of 'soil' than we would probably wish for at average, given a chance. While some struggle with the hardship of soil ph. to adulthood, some are just as lucky to have be born in the right 'soil'. But all of us compete for same goals, dreams and ambitions, with limited opportunities and resources.

Psychologist believes that milestones development is an important and critical way for measuring a child's progress in several aspect of life as it acts as a checkpoint in child's development to determine what the average child is capable of doing at a particular age.

Eliud Kichoge is arguably the best long-distance runner of his generation. He attributes his success not as an immediate one, but one which came after a lot of efforts and sacrifices. Perhaps what many people around the world don't know about Kipchoge is that he comes from a very humble background and began small. Many know him by so many tittles and world records tracks that he recorded in long distance races, but little is known about his personal life. The son of a struggling single mother started to shine in 1999 while at Kaptel secondary school where he also made tremendous efforts in athletics. Since then, Kipchoge has always led a simple life. One of the local newspapers in Kenya once recorded, "Kipchoge is anything but ordinary", in reference to his normal routine and high discipline in his early morning trainings.

Eliud Kipchoge was born on 5 November 1984 in a small village of Kapsisiywa, Nandi County in Kenya. Being the last-born child in a family of four, he would spend most of his time with his mother over the weekends and during school holidays. In 2019, his old school, Kaptel High school hit the headlines as one of its most celebrated alumni made the INEOS challenge a dream come true and proofed to the world that indeed **no human is limited**. Kaptel turns out to be the only school around that time where Kipchoge's dream would later be transformed. Established in 1968, Kaptel high school first students were village boys who spent most of their days hawking milk. In a similar occasion, a local newspaper recorded a number of these boys from very humble backgrounds to have passed the test of

time and was now 'the big boys' in the government. Among them includes; Bernard Langat who is a Kenyan-born American long distance runner, former Agriculture minister Willy Bett, sports department CEO in Nandi County, Kennedy Cheruiyot, senior commutations lecturer, Dr. Abraham Kiprop, member of parliament, Hon. Elijah Langat, a medic in Heidelberg Germany, Dr. Elly Kibet and Dr. Philemon Langat who is based in Illinois, USA among many other successful men from the school.

During this time, Eliud Kipchoge had never proceeded beyond Zonal schools' games competition, which is equivalent to a division level. This was the time he would take his bicycle and ride over sixty kilometers a day to sell milk in Kapsabet town. Occasionally, Kipchoge had to travel for two miles to and fro school where he graduated in 1999, but did not took athletics seriously by then.

He would then later in 2001, meet his trainer

and coach, Patrick Sang who is a former Olympic medalist in steeplechase. Kipchoge was around sixteen years old then.

What is that one lesson that we can learn from this little, humbling story of Kipchoge? Well, often than always, we even become strangers in our own lives, but perseveres are destined for greatness. Perhaps you may have heard of the famous Hellen Keller and her condition. The story of Keller and her teacher, Anne Sullivan, was made famous by Keller's autobiography, **'The story of my life'**. At nineteen months old, Keller contracted an unknown illness, prescribed by doctors as 'an acute congestion of the stomach and the brain'. This illness left her both deaf and blind. She would later record on her autobiography how this illness changed her life as, 'Sea in a dense fog'. Despite all these series of events, Keller was able to attend school at Perkins institute for the Blind in 1894 and became the first deaf-blind person to earn a Bachelor of Arts degree.

Keller is forever remembered for her message of optimism, of hope, of good cheer and of loving service to humanity. This massage will linger longer with those who were fortunate enough to have received it. Many would want to believe that we live in a world where things would not happen the way we want them to be or think it will be. This often leads to a psychological state of mind known as 'cognitive dissonance'. Keller often spoke of the joy that life gave her. She was thankful for the abilities that she did possessed and at one time stated that the most productive pleasures she had were; curiosity and imagination. Imagine this little gift that we often take for granted while we are still alive. Imagine what a short distance run in the morning could do for your health. In one of his interviews, Kipchoge told the journalist that 'everyone should embrace sports, that a little run in the morning scares the doctor way'.

It goes without saying that the world is changed not by those superior, but those who are determine to fight to the very end and leads a sacrificial life, even that child of a peasant man. A practical example includes; Nelson Mandela, Churchill Winston and Barrack Obama. All these individuals portray an important aspect of leaving a legacy behind, that's selflessness. Keller in particular insinuates that, 'helping your fellow men were one's only excuse for being in this world and in the doing of things to help one's fellows, lay the secret of lasting happiness'. And so back to our psychological concept of 'milestones development', what really is it that defines what we become. Is it the food that we eat or the schools that we attend? I always believe that there is a place for every man who is alive today, somehow there has to be. And so, depending on whatever soil that you were born in, it really doesn't matter, still there is a place for you. I am a great football fan and often times when we gather with other boys of my age to watch a match and for this matter English premier league or champion's league. Many of my friends will put comments and lament of how bad lack indeed that they were born in the wrong soil, Africa. They always wish they would have been born in Britain or States where they always convince me that it is 'the soil of opportunities. As to whether that is true or not, I don't know for sure. Perhaps they are right, but how do you explain the magical African players playing in the same arena with players from 'the right soil'? This takes us back to my first point, that there is always a place for every man alive today, none is limited. When I look at the magical Sadio Mane of Senegal, Mohammed Salah of Egypt and Macdonald Mariga of Kenya playing the English premier league, I always ask myself from which soil did these men came from. Yet when I look at their individual backgrounds, they have emerged from very humble backgrounds and today they are not just worth millions of Euros, but they are equally worldwide celebrated heroes. Recently, a CEO of a multibillion company in Kenya, Bob Collymore passed away. What is interesting is that many people did not realize that Collymore had no university degree during all this time as a CEO, till his point of death. Many knew him by the companies' remarkable success which is largely attributed to him. Yet when I look at his background, I see a man who just realized that there was a place for him, somewhat. From being the only black student in a class full of white rich kids, he fought for what he believed was rightfully his, even without a university degree, he was outstanding. It is almost impossible to conclude that one thing contributes a lot in what we become than the other. But one thing for sure that we can learn from the short stories of these individuals is **attitude.** Do you believe you're in the right soil? I bet you do, but if you don't, you'd better think again. What is interesting is that even in the world's driest desserts, you'll find trees that have stand out and have adapted to the environment. What is that thing that is limiting you from reaching your goals? Is it the soil, the friends that you interact with or could it be your very self? I have heard it said that man is the greatest enemy of himself. Whatever it is that is limiting you, you always have control over it. Kipchoge's life is not just interesting, but inspiring too. He lives his generation with a legacy, became eye opener to many. He lives in the Great

Rift Valley province where he continues to inspire the lives of locals. In a recent occasion, President Uhuru Kenyatta honored him with Elder of the Order of the Golden Heart, EGH award during a national holiday function. He is married to Grace Sugut and blessed with three children. Kipchoge believes that there is a place for him too. He didn't allow the kind of school that he attended define his fate. Neither did he allow the status of his family social background nor do economic statuses define his dreams. Later on, in his life, his coach and all-time mentor would comment on Kipchoge's simplicity nature that besides being a worldwide figure in athletics, he never changed his training ground to at least advanced facility. He continued his training in the village grassroots and supports the upcoming athletes from his homeland. Again, this is the aspect of selflessness and remaining focus on the goals. I have also heard

it said more than once of individuals and especially politicians who have started from humble background, but once they have reached their 'destiny', they change their lifestyles and sadly this often marks the beginning of their downfall.

It is one thing to go up and another to come down. Successful people would always wake up every morning with a desire of always wanting to be better the next day. Sometimes we set goals for ourselves that even scares us and we begin to doubt if we are worth fighting for them. A writer once said "your own idea bores you". Once in college, I always asked myself if the course I was taking was worth the sleepless nights I had to sacrifice during exams time. And so, in our battles we feel like giving up and fight other battles that don't belongs to us. The naked truth is that we always have that role model that we look up to all the times. It's equally true that we may have people around us who secretly admire our success however small it may be. It could be at school or workplace, there is always that one person who feels encouraged in our presence, in that board meeting or in that end of year examination results. It may also be at family level. Now imagine giving up on our battles…We do not just let down ourselves, but we also let down those around us and those looking up to us. When we win, they can proudly say, 'me too'. I'd like to personally identify with the Obama's slogan, **'yes we can'**. We can because together we are strong, we've got the synergy. My bishop once told me that even in our religious life, we are what we are in faith not because of anything else, but because at least someone took the time to teach us the word of God. Someone took time to pray for you, it could have been someone you never got to meet. Or it could have been your great great grandparents. What matters is that somehow, your life has been influenced by others all through.

How many of us like rewards? It is human nature to always seek reward because in a way, our brains are wired to seek the positive rewards which makes us feel good. The reason why I am motivated to talk about reward at this point is that, often comes a reward after a good job. But at what level in life do we really begin to pursue rewards? I remember since I was a toddler, my mum would always give me conditions for a reward. She would say,' if you don't cry, I'll buy you chocolate'. One thing however, that I came to realize is that as we grow up, we tend to bargain for even bigger rewards. This is brought about by a mere fact that our goals become clearer and expectations together with responsibilities become challenging with time. But what happen when our efforts seem unnoticed and no reward

Seems to be coming through? Worst is when the reward goes to the wrong person and this happens often times. Can you imagine what a national football team goes through when they have to spent the night sleeping on the floor at the airport when they have a match the following day? Or an athlete who has been through hell training day and night misses a visa for Olympic Games in a foreign country? These are challenges that are true and often no one talks about them. I followed with great concern a number of brilliant children from humble backgrounds that could not proceed to secondary school due to lack of school fees. I listen and reasoned with them as they shared their dreams dying while they are young. I am not that rich myself, but I imagine a dream inside of me dying slowly not because I am not qualified, but because I can't afford the fee. I remember reading a journal while in high school that said, 'Why the work of a

Starving artist needs to die'. Yet I thought because someone knew the producer, their script is taken. But my question is, isn't that the world that we live in today?

Have you ever asked yourself why do so many youths round the world end up in drugs and substance abuse; is it that our governments have got no rewards for our degrees and brilliant minds fresh from college? Being a youth always comes with optimism and anxiety of what the future holds. We always expect huge rewards as well. The employer says 'no, but you've got no experience'. The youths say, 'no I've got knowledge and new ideas. In midst of all this, times flies and before you realize, your reward is gone.

The early stages of life are the time when we write our story, our legacy. That notwithstanding, do not all together allow your past to determine what the future holds for you. Always wake up with a positive mind and tell yourself that there is always a place for you, no matter what. Have the desire to always improve every day and begin to break your limits. Remember your reward is just due on time, when it finally arrives embrace and help others get to their destiny. Also remember, a run in the morning scares the doctor away.

STANDING OUT AND CHOOSING THE RIGHT TEAM

In the previous chapter, I began by sharing that I am a great football fan. I imagine the kind of feeling that fans always go through especially when their team is not performing well. Outside football, look around you. What is that one school, hospital or a company that inspires you? My point is, when we have a good team of players, we don't just win the match, but we equally inspire the rest of the world. From that point in life that you choose a career to when you live to it, you always need the right team to get you there. What kind of people or friends surrounds your life circle? But why does the people that we interact with matters so much in what we become? One of my professors once told me," if the character of a woman you aspire to date isn't clear, look around her friends". This, I came to realize that no man or woman can really conform to a certain group of friends unless they share something in common. Have you ever made an effort in life to mingle with people who challenge your ideas, who really challenge you to upgrade the game? Successful entrepreneurs for example, cannot at one point be found buying the ideas of street idle minds, rather they venture into friendships and connections that challenge them to strive to even higher goals. As the saying goes, 'garbage in, garbage out' so is it true with our minds. When we don't challenge our minds to think and solve problems, they remain dormant and we begin to simply lose focus and, in the end, loose hope altogether.

So how do we actually stand out? In our previous chapter, we have examined early lives of certain individuals like Hellen Keller, Bob Collymore and Eliud Kipchoge. Standing out is totally different from living in isolation, no. In fact, it is always advisable for one to always mingle with people as much as possible during one's life time. So, if at any point you find yourself in a public transport, pick ideas, engage in a talk and keep a light moment.

Eliud Kipchoge's unparalleled remarkable victory in marathon reached another level when he became the first human in history to run a sub-two-hour marathon as part of INEOS 1:59 challenge. Later after the run, Kipchoge confirmed to the press that the success of his run had very much to do with his team. So, what does this really mean? Well, it is not just enough to have a good team when we don't come out ourselves and do the real work. This means that we should take full control of our team and playing our part, this way we stand out. Depending on what field that you are in, there are always structured ways and steps that one needs to employ when considering the right team for you. The first thing that you need to do is to assess the distance between you and them. How far are they from you? Can you reach them or are they available when you need them? Individuals need to be usually available and I mean usually especially when you need to reach them and to act immediately. Secondly, they should have same interest, same ambitions and same vision with you. This way, the notion of 'if I lose, we lose' becomes the foundation of your relationships and each member of the team will be committed since if the team loses, he or she also loses. Thirdly, ask yourself if you are the one leading the team. If the answer is yes, ask yourself the following questions; can you lead by example? Do you have what it takes?

Once you have assessed the three aspects above, truly listen to your team members and always trust the process and avoid shortcuts.

NO HUMAN IS LIMITED

The events of 12th October 2019 INEOS challenge really inspired and moved me to write this little story which I am hoping would equally inspire someone as well. Ineos 1:59 challenge was successful, the event featuring Kenyan athlete Eliud Kipchoge. A communication company in Kenya, Safaricom announced a free YouTube bundles for Eliud Kipchoge's INEOS challenge from 8a.m to 4p.m same day. Eliud Kipchoge attracted four million, nine hundred thousand YouTube views on marathon challenge on that day. More than five hundred million views were recorded in total from over two hundred territories while others tuned in through various other channels. One lesson of course that we can learn from Eliud is that no human is limited. He has not just said it himself, but has just proofed it beyond reasonable doubt. Always human beings have set standards to what and what cannot be achieved leaving them to live ordinary life and fail to attempt even the wild ideas that we live with them every day.

We are living in a generation where we always desire for instant gratification and success. The truth of the matter is that the good things takes time. It has taken nearly sixty-five years to proof that a man can run a marathon in less than two hours. This is a lesson that teaches us to be patient enough to go through the process because God makes everything beautiful in the fullness of time.

It is actually worth noting that success is communal. I was in Nairobi city when Kipchoge was running the marathon and it really touched my heart deeply how the people came together to watch the race live at Kenyatta International Conference Centre. In fact, after the marathon, the whole world went into frenzy.

How was it to see a single man raised up by a single mother bringing the world together? When you win, the community wins and before you realize, you'll be surprised how many people will be celebrating your success. It would altogether be unfair if I do not talk about the pacemakers. I am equally pretty sure that Kipchoge will be much disappointed if I don't talk about his pacemakers that helped him win the race. I watched with great concern how they hysterically clapped when he did cross the finish line. They represent the true friends that we all need in our journey to be successful. Each of us needs that person or team who will genuinely want what's best for us and would equally be ecstatic when we win.

Made in the USA
Monee, IL
30 November 2025

36872526R00023